Prairie
Birds

PRAIRIE
BIRDS

CHRIS C. FISHER

LONE
PINE

The Publisher
Lone Pine Publishing

206, 10426–81 Avenue	202A, 1110 Seymour St.	16149 Redmond Way, #180
Edmonton, Alberta	Vancouver, BC	Redmond, Washington
Canada T6E 1X5	Canada V6B 3N3	U.S.A. 98052

Canadian Cataloguing in Publication Data
Fisher, Chris, 1970–
     Prairie birds

Includes bibliographical references and index.
ISBN 1-55105-051 X

     1. Birds—Prairie Provinces—Identification. 2. Bird watching—Prairie Provinces. 3. Large type books. I. Title.
QL685.5.P7F57 1995   598.29712   C95-9110893-6

Senior Editor: *Nancy Foulds*
Project Editor: *Roland Lines*
Design & Layout: *Bruce Timothy Keith, Greg Brown*
Colour Illustrations: *Gary Ross, Ewa Pluciennik, Joan Johnston,*
                    Kitty Ho, Beata Kurpinski
Black & White Illustrations: *Donna McKinnon*
Cover Illustration: *Gary Ross*
Separations and Film: *Elite Lithographers Co. Ltd., Edmonton, Alberta*
Printing: *Quebecor Jasper Printing Inc., Edmonton, Alberta, Canada*

The Publisher gratefully acknowledges the support of the National Library of Canada, Alberta Community Development, the Department of Canadian Heritage and the Canada/Alberta Agreement on the cultural industries.

Acknowledgements

A book of this nature relies on the contributions and generosity of many talented people. Special thanks go to the early ornithologists and naturalists of the prairies, whose tireless studies and observations advanced the science and the appreciation of prairie birds, providing the foundation for future generations of bird enthusiasts. To Gary Ross and Ewa Pluciennik, whose illustrations have elevated the quality of this book beyond the limited medium of the written page. To Carole Patterson for her continual support, and to Robin Bovey, Nancy Baron and Gerry McKeating for their guidance with the text. Many thanks to the team at Lone Pine Publishing—Shane Kennedy, Roland Lines and Nancy Foulds—for their input, advice and steering. Finally, my thanks go to John Acorn, for his guidance and revisions, and to Dr. Jim Butler, whose passion for the natural world fosters the communication of wilderness values.

Contents

Water Birds

Long-legged Birds

Birds of Prey

Game Birds

Black Birds

Crow, Blackbirds,
Starling, Grackle... 64

Mid-sized Birds

Robin, Blue Jay,
Meadowlark, Magpie... 70

Small Showy Birds

Chickadee, Swallows, Warbler, Buntings... 85

Small Brown Birds

Sparrows, Wrens,
Flycatcher, Vireo... 98

Introduction

Birds are colourful, abundant and unavoidable characters in our lives, and they naturally arouse our curiosity. This book is not intended to serve solely as a bird identification guide but also as a bird appreciation guide. By connecting a name to a bird we satisfy our urge to identify, which begins our introduction to the lifestyle and habits of a dynamic creature. Once a species is formally introduced, an unconventional relationship ensues between the bird and the birder, a relationship that continues to develop over a lifetime of meetings.

This book presents only a brief introduction into the lives of prairie birds, but the information contained within forces you to take on a different perspective on the natural world. As ducks become known to you as Mallards,

Pintails or Shovelers, for example, you will establish relationships with the birds. Their songs will sound sweeter, their plumage will look brighter, and their hardships will no longer be discounted out of ignorance.

The 90 species described in this guide represent many of the common species found on the prairies. This book doesn't comprehensively represent all prairie birds, nor is it simply about the ones you are most likely to encounter. Instead, the selection of birds described here present a balance between the familiar and the noteworthy.

The bird descriptions in this book are generalized for three provinces and three states—Alberta, Saskatchewan, Manitoba, Montana, North Dakota and South Dakota—and as a result, the abundance and distribution of the species, which naturally vary from place to

place, cannot be described with total accuracy. There is no one site where all these birds will appear simultaneously; however, most of these species can be observed—at least seasonally—within a few hours' drive of most major centres.

Many of the smaller birds are difficult to observe in the wild, but fortunately they're fairly distinctive in their songs. Most birds have characteristic songs—an enviable adaptation to resolve territorial and personal disputes with others of their species. Many recordings are available to learn these songs. Where it was feasible, a catchy paraphrase of a song is included in the descriptions to help you identify bird songs. This technique of birdwatching by identifying songs is gaining in popularity, since listening for birds is often more efficient, productive and rewarding than waiting for a visual confirmation.

Although this guide is primarily meant to inspire you into personal experiences with birds, if you are unable to do this it's hoped that this book will itself provide some experience of the lives of our prairie birds. The descriptive text for each bird will help you identify birds in the field, but more importantly it personalizes each bird's unique character. It's important to realize that although the birds' actions and features are personified in the descriptions, since their instinctive actions are easier to relate to in this manner, to expect their behaviour to mimic ours undermines the complexities of a bird's life.

Far too many of the bird species described in this book are threatened. That doesn't represent a bias in the selection of species, but rather it's a direct reflection of the current health of the prairie ecosystem. By increasing the awareness and appreciation of prairie birds, naturalists will either continue to watch the decline in many species, or they will strive passionately for conservation programs to maintain our valued relationships with them.

The Organization of This Book

Many existing bird guides are bulky, and they can be confusing to novice birdwatchers, frustrating them to the point that they put down the guide rather than satisfy their natural curiosity. This book, because of its inherent simplicity, presents the birds in eight groups based on physical or behavioural similarities. It purposefully doesn't follow a tight taxonomic order, which can be very confusing for beginners. Most birds that are seen in the backyard, at the cabin or along highways will be found in this book.

Waterbirds

Ducks, Geese, Pelican, Gulls, etc. This large, diverse group represents birds that have webbed feet and are commonly seen on the water in lakes and marshes. Although geese, gulls and terns are often seen great distances from water, their general appearance ties them closely with this group.

Long-legged Birds

Crane, Herons and Shorebirds. Many of these birds are waders, which are often seen standing in knee-deep water, while others are more often seen in open grasslands. All of the birds in this category tend to have proportionately longer legs than most birds.

Birds of Prey

Hawks, Eagle, Owls, Nighthawk, etc. Birds of this group are readily identified by their talons, powerful bills and forward-facing eyes, despite the great difference in size between the largest eagle and the smallest falcon. Although the Common Nighthawk is not related to hawks or owls, it resembles an owl when it's perched, and it resembles a falcon in flight.

Game Birds

Pheasant, Partridge and Grouse. The three species of this group, which are all distantly related to domestic poultry, are best identified by their short, low flights, stocky chicken-like bodies and close association with the ground.

Black Birds

Crow, Blackbirds, Starling, Grackle, etc. This is a grouping of unrelated birds whose base colour is predominantly black. It's important to realize that although all these birds are black, they're not all 'blackbirds.'

Mid-sized Birds

Robin, Blue Jay, Meadowlark, Magpie, etc. The birds of this grouping are sized between a robin and a magpie. Many have distinctive songs and plumages, which helps in their identification.

Small Showy Birds

Chickadee, Swallows, Warbler, Buntings, etc. These small birds are grouped together on the basis of size and colour. All of them are smaller than a robin, and they have bold plumages of more than one dominant colour.

Small Brown Birds

Sparrows, Wrens, Flycatcher, Vireo, etc. These small birds all have fairly indistinct plumages. They're all predominantly brown or olive in colour, and they're smaller than a robin. Their songs are often very useful in identification.

Habitats

When birdwatching, the first thing to note is the habitat you are exploring, so you will know what kinds of birds to expect—ducks are found in ponds and marshes, herons on shorelines and woodpeckers in woods. You won't find a grouse in the water or a loon up a tree. Each of the birds in this book is accompanied by one or more icons to identify the habitat(s) in which you are likely to find it.

The native prairie grasslands have all but disappeared, replaced by farmland, which is now so much a part of the prairie landscape, and by our towns and cities. Nevertheless, there are remaining areas of semi-natural prairie where Red-tailed Hawks hunt for small mammals and American Goldfinches forage for seed. The Gray Partridge also prefers this type of grassland, and small coveys of these birds will often explode into the air before gliding away to disappear in the short grass cover again. In winter, Snowy Owls and Snow Buntings forage over the frozen ground. This is not a habitat that teems with birds, but it can provide worthwhile birdwatching expeditions.

Woodland habitats are much favoured by many bird species. Deciduous or mixed woods are usually best for birdwatching. They provide a wide variety of habitat types within the forest, and many birds are attracted to the dense understorey of shrubs found in some areas. Many birds nest in woodlands, including Black-capped Chickadees, Yellow Warblers, Black-billed Magpies, House Wrens, White-throated Sparrows, Downy Woodpeckers and some of the predatory birds, such as Red-tailed Hawks and Great Horned Owls. Riverine woodlands often occur in river valleys cut into prairie grasslands, and balsam poplar and cottonwood trees are common there. They are often the most natural and best city birdwatching areas. Conifer-dominated woodlands are often found on the colder, north-facing slopes of a river valley. The tree canopy is often denser here, and there is less of a shrub layer. As a result, the birds are harder to see in the dense tree cover.

Any habitat where there is open water or even a damp marshy area is attractive to all sorts of birds. Some birds, such as ducks and geese, feed and breed in these habitats, while others come to drink and bathe. Willows often dominate the vegetation surrounding these areas, and a close look will reveal a variety of birds. One of the best wetland habitats for birdwatching is the slough, where there are likely to be Red-winged Blackbirds and many species of ducks in the reeds and cattails. Artificial ponds and lakes in city parks are also used by birds as long as there is a semi-natural shore with surrounding vegetation.

The more formal city parks and residential backyards are by no means natural habitats, but they are still used by some birds, most notably robins, magpies, starlings and sparrows.

Habitat Icons

The habitat with which a bird is associated is often a useful clue to both its identification and its ecological role. Each bird in this guide is accompanied by at least one habitat symbol, which represents a general habitat where this bird is most likely to be observed. However, vagrant and migrating birds can turn up in just about any habitat type. Although novice naturalists may be frustrated by this, these unexpected surprises are among the most powerful motivations for the increasing legion of birdwatchers.

Grasslands and Fields

Wetlands

Manicured Residential Parks

Gardens, Feeders

Mixed Woods

Open Riverine Valleys

Shrubs and Thickets

Lakes

Mallard *Anas platyrhynchos*

The Mallard is the classic duck of the prairies—the male's iridescent green head and chestnut breast are symbolic of wetland habitat. This large duck is commonly seen feeding in prairie potholes, small lakes, farmers' fields and, during the winter, along river edges. With their legs beneath the middle part of their bodies, Mallards walk easily, and they can spring straight out of the water into flight without a running start.

In spring, the male Mallards pursue the females energetically, but a male will abandon his mate soon after she's laid eggs. This lack of paternal commitment may seem harsh, but in fact it's beneficial to the female and the ducklings. A colourful father would likely attract the attention of predators, placing the lives of the well-camouflaged female and ducklings at risk.

Northern Pintail

Anas acuta

The Northern Pintail is the most elegant duck on the prairies. As its name suggests, the tail feathers of this large duck taper to form a slender, elongated tail. Adding to the sleek appearance of the male Northern Pintail is its graceful neck, which has a white stripe extending up the back to the base of the chocolate-brown head.

Like the Mallard, the Northern Pintail is a puddle duck, and it's well adapted to life on land and in shallow water. When it feeds in shallow wetlands and prairie potholes, this dabbler often 'tips up,' submerging its head and neck and extending its graceful tail skyward.

Blue-winged Teal

Anas discors

The male Blue-winged Teal has a thin, white crescent on its cheek and a grey-blue head to match the inner wing patches. These small ducks are extremely swift flyers, which frustrates their many predators.

Unlike many of the larger prairie dabblers, which migrate only as far as necessary, teals overwinter in Central and South America. For this reason Blue-winged Teals are often the last ducks to arrive on the prairies in spring and the first to leave in autumn, usually by the end of September. On average, the smaller species of waterfowl migrate further than the larger varieties.

American Wigeon *Anas americana*

The male American Wigeon looks and sounds somewhat like an old timer—the white forehead and grey sides of this medium-sized duck's head look like a balding scalp, and the slow, nasal *wee-he-he-he-he* call sounds like a wheezing laugh. Broad green patches extend back from the male's eyes, almost as if his laughing brought tears to his eyes and caused his green mascara to run.

Like the other dabbling ducks of the prairies, American Wigeons lay about 10 eggs in a well-concealed nest. The female incubates the eggs for 25 days before the ducklings begin to hatch. The ducklings leave the nest almost immediately and grow quickly—in 50 days the first of the young begin to fly. Owing to this short rearing period, prairie ducks can often raise two clutches of young in a year.

Northern Shoveler *Anas clypeata*

The Northern Shoveler is very well named, for its bill stands out among prairie ducks. The large flat bill of this dabbler has comb-like structures along the edges, which allows it to strain small plants and invertebrates from the water surface or from muddy substrates. The Northern Shoveler, which is often seen lounging in knee-deep water, carries its cumbersome bill proudly.

Although the male Northern Shoveler has a green head and is of a similar size, don't confuse him with a Mallard. The Northern Shoveler's oversized bill, chestnut sides and white breast clearly separate it from the chestnut-breasted Mallard.

Lesser Scaup *Aythya affinis*

The Lesser Scaup is the Oreo cookie of the prairie ducks—black at both ends and white in the middle. In prairie potholes and lakes, this scaup is among the most common of the diving ducks.

Unlike dabbling ducks, diving ducks have their legs placed well back on their body. This is advantageous for underwater swimming, but it makes walking difficult. All ducks are front heavy, so for diving ducks to stand they must raise their front ends high to maintain their balance. As a result, Lesser Scaups are clumsy on land, but they regain their dignity when they take to the water.

Ruddy Duck *Oxyura jamaicensis*

The clowns of prairie wetlands, Ruddy Ducks are truly charming. As they energetically paddle around their breeding wetlands, the males display with great vigour, beating their breasts with their bright blue beaks. The *plap-plap-plap-plap-plap* of their display increases in speed to the crescendo—a spasmodic jerk and sputter. The male's performance occurs in the open water of prairie potholes from April to the middle of June. As it struts around wetlands with its tail fully cocked, the small, reddish male displays the arrogance of an animal many times its size.

Canvasback *Aythya valisineria*

Their rich red heads add to the stately air of Canvasbacks. In the lakes and potholes where they breed, these large ducks tend to occupy the central area, diving deeply to forage for plants and aquatic invertebrates. They're very well named, as no other red-headed duck has an all white back.

Despite its field marks, the Canvasback is easily and often confused with the Redhead, a duck that shares its breeding ponds. Unlike the Canvasback the Redhead has a grey back and a prominent forehead. The Canvasback's bill is unique to prairie ducks—it slopes straight from the top of the head to the tip of the bill.

American Coot

Fulica americana

The highly successful 'mud hen' of the prairies is a delightful mix of confusion and comedy. The American Coot has the lobed toes of a grebe, the bill of a chicken and the black body of a duck. However, the American Coot is not remotely related to any of these species—its closest prairie cousins are the rails and cranes.

American Coots are often seen chugging along in shallow prairie wetlands, their heads bobbing in synchrony with their paddling feet. As a coot's swimming speed increases so does the back and forth motion of its head. At peak speed this motion appears to disorient American Coots, since they prefer to fake a take-off and run and flap to the other side of the wetland.

Red-necked Grebe *Podiceps grisegena*

Red-necked Grebes court with fanfare. During April and May the cacophony of their wails, cackles and laughs is the loudest sound on prairie lakes. Their white cheeks, red neck and flared cranial crest complement the vocal display.

These large grebes can be seen on smaller lakes and in the protected bays of larger lakes throughout the northern prairies. The size of the wetland is important because Red-necked Grebes need 50 to 60 metres of open water to get up enough speed for take-off. They never stray far from water, and they build a floating nest and eat small fish, invertebrates and tadpoles.

Western Grebe

Aechmophorus occidentalis

The spectacular courtship of these black and white grebes is unique to the prairies. It's a complex visual display that involves both sexes and ensures that the pair's bond is fully established. In the 'weed dance,' the pair rise gently out of the water and caress each other with aquatic plants held in their rapier-like bills. 'Rushing,' the climax of the visual ritual, is repeated frequently by the pair. During this phase the birds glance knowingly at one another and then explode into a sprint. Both grebes stand high, wings held back and heads cocked, and dash across the water until their small legs give out, driving them into a head-first dive.

Horned Grebe *Podiceps auritus*

This small grebe is common on prairie potholes, but it's often overlooked because of its drab, unassuming lifestyle. Although it lacks the personality and colour of the larger prairie grebes, the Horned Grebe shares many of the same behavioural and physical characteristics.

All grebes have the strange habit of eating feathers, occasionally packing their digestive tracts. One explanation is that grebes use the feathers to dislodge the bones and scales of their fishy prey from their digestive tracts. Grebes also have very unusual feet. Unlike the fully webbed toes of ducks, gulls and pelicans, the toes of grebes are individually lobed, not webbed.

Canada Goose

Branta canadensis

Just like the leaves on the trees, Canada Geese are indicators of the changing seasons. Their magnificent spring and autumn migrations touch most prairie residents. Even people locked up in cities can't ignore the resonant honking that drifts down from their V-shaped flocks.

The many resident Canada Geese that choose to nest in the northern prairies are among the largest in North America. Short migrations and bountiful food resources often enable these large birds to raise two clutches a year. Breeding pairs are regal in appearance and legendarily loyal. They mate for life, and not only will a widowed goose often remain unpaired for the rest of its life, it's also common for a mate to remain at the side of a fallen partner.

Snow Goose

Chen caerulescens

One of the great spectacles of nature is the spring migration of Snow Geese through the prairies. These large white birds fuel up on prairie waste grain before continuing their northern migration to their Arctic breeding grounds. Their staging areas are often in farmlands closely associated with large, shallow wetlands.

Anyone who has seen tens of thousands of snow geese lifting in unison won't soon forget the experience—their black-tipped wings contrast with their clean white plumage to create a cloud of life. Snow Geese yelp noisily, and they fly in loose, wavy lines instead of the well-formed 'V's of Canada Geese.

Tundra Swan *Cygnus columbianus*

Small flocks of this large white bird are common throughout the northern prairies in April. Although they don't migrate in large complex flocks like Snow Geese, their individual splendour dwarfs all other waterfowl.

Unlike all other large white birds on the prairies, swans don't have black wing tips. The only contrasts with their all-white plumage are their black bills, feet and eyes, and their small yellow 'tears.' Tundra Swans commonly stand on frozen wetlands during spring and autumn, and they hold their heads high atop their long, graceful necks.

American White Pelican *Pelecanus erythrorhynchos*

Almost everyone can accurately identify a pelican, but many inexperienced naturalists assume that they're restricted to tropical regions. This is unfortunate because the core breeding range of the American White Pelican lies within the prairie region.

Several factors must exist for a large prairie lake to support a pelican colony. Most important is an abundant supply of fish in the vicinity of the colony. Pelicans also need low islands that remain free of harassment for their breeding colonies, because they're extremely sensitive to human disturbances. Although this distinctive bird was severely persecuted in the past, an appreciation of its needs has brought many American White Pelicans back to our larger prairie lakes.

Double-crested Cormorant

Phalacrocorax auritus

The Double-crested Cormorant is the only cormorant of the prairies, and it nests in trees or alongside pelicans on low islands. Somewhere along the evolutionary process cormorants lost, or never acquired, the ability to waterproof their wings, and these large black waterbirds patiently dry their wings after each swim. They're often seen perched with their wings partially spread to expose their wet feathers to the sun and wind.

It would seem to be a great disadvantage for a water bird to have to dry its wings, but the cormorant's wetable feathers decrease its buoyancy, which makes it easier to swim after the fish on which it preys. Sealed nostrils, a long, rudder-like tail and excellent underwater vision also complement the Double-crested Cormorant's aquatic lifestyle.

Ring-billed Gull Larus delawarensis

This is the common 'seagull' of prairie cities. It breeds mainly in landlocked areas and sees the ocean primarily during the winter months. These familiar birds have adapted well to modern agricultural processes, urban development and waste disposal.

Although Ring-billed Gulls are a daily sight in prairie towns and cities, they nest in large colonies in sparsely vegetated marshes, beaches and islands. Most Ring-billed Gulls leave the prairies in late November and return after a five-month coastal retreat.

Franklin's Gull

Larus pipixcan

These small, black-headed gulls shy away from city life. Colonies of up to 40,000 birds build their floating nests atop piled reeds in shallow water. Franklin's gulls are often seen flying above large prairie marshes, or they follow a farmer's plow and snatch up exposed worms and dead mice. They have long been appreciated by prairie farmers for their ravenous appetite for grasshoppers. Franklin's gull was named to honour Sir John Franklin, the Arctic explorer who died while trying to find the Northwest Passage.

Common Tern *Sterna hirundo*

The Common Tern generally goes unnoticed until a splash draws attention to its head-first dive into the water. Once it has firmly seized a small fish in its black-tipped bill, the tern bounces back into the air and continues its leisurely flight.

Although terns and gulls share many of the same physical characteristics, there are several features that clearly separate these two groups. Terns seldom rest on the water, and they rarely soar in flight. In addition, terns have very short necks, and they tend to look towards the ground during flight. These characteristics should help identify the Common Tern, whose black cap doesn't extend below the eye.

Black Tern *Chlidonias niger*

In mid-flight this black aerial acrobat has the agility to catch elusive dragonflies and to snatch aquatic insects from the water's surface. Like large swallows, Black Terns dip and spin in mid-air as though in defiance of the laws of flight that restrict most other birds. These incredible manoeuvres can be observed over the marshes, sloughs and small lakes where these terns feed. Black Terns nest in similar areas, and they usually build a raised nest in dense cattails.

In order to spell this tern's scientific name correctly, one must misspell *chelidonias*, the Greek word for 'swallow.' When the Black Tern was first described and named, the author accidentally left out the 'e,' a mistake that must be repeated for the name to be correct.

Sandhill Crane

Grus canadensis

Although these large birds don't nest on the prairies, they're often seen during their spring and autumn migrations. Sandhill Cranes often fly in large V-shaped flocks, which can cause them to be misidentified as Canada Geese, but the Sandhill Crane's rattling call is distinctly different from the Canada Goose's honk.

Long before the first wave of Sandhill Cranes appears on the horizon, the flock's slow rattling announces its presence. Although Sandhill Cranes seldom flap their wings, the great flocks move quickly by using the thermal lift of the prairie landscape. During peak migratory periods, waves of passing cranes can fill whole mornings with their rattles.

Great Blue Heron

Ardea herodias

The Great Blue Heron is one of the largest prairie birds. It often stands motionless, like a lone sentry, as it surveys the calm waters of a prairie wetland. Its graceful lines blend naturally with the dancing grasses and cattails along the shore.

Great Blue Herons are often mistaken for Sandhill Cranes, which are of similar size and colour. However, the Great Blue Heron holds its long neck curved back in an 'S' during flight and often while it's hunting—in preparation for a sudden strike. Also, Great Blue Herons, which nest in colonies in trees, are seen on the prairies during summer, when cranes are nesting far to the north. Great Blue Herons rarely appear in great numbers away from their nesting colonies, because they prefer to hunt alone or in small, evenly spaced groups.

Black-crowned Night Heron *Nycticorax nycticorax*

This hawk-sized heron is far less conspicuous than its great blue cousin. As its name suggests, the Black-crowned Night Heron prefers to hunt for frogs and small fish in shallow wetlands during the evening hours—a habit that likely leads to low estimates of the abundance of this heron.

Despite the hours it keeps, Black-crowned Night Herons are occasionally seen in large numbers. At larger prairie wetlands surrounded by dense shrubs, colonies of Black-crowned Night Herons thrive, and in places such as these it's not uncommon to observe the twilight activities of over 20 birds.

Killdeer
Charadrius vociferus

The Killdeer is probably the most familiar shorebird of the prairies. It nests on gravelly shorelines, utility rights-of-way, lawns and pastures, and occasionally on gravel roofs in cites. Its name is a paraphrase of its distinctive loud call, *kill-dee-dee kill-dee-dee kill-deer*, and not an indication of its hunting habits.

The Killdeer's response to predators relies on deception and good acting skills. To divert a predator's attention away from a nest or a brood of young, an adult Killdeer will flop around to feign an injury (usually a broken wing or leg). Once the Killdeer has the attention of the fox, coyote or hawk, it leads the predator away from the vulnerable nest. Once a safe distance is reached, the adult Killdeer is suddenly healed and flies off, leaving the predator confused and hungry.

Common Snipe
Gallinago gallinago

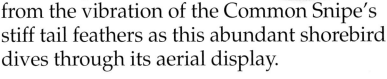

On warm spring evenings an eerie, rapid *who-who-who-who* can be heard over many prairie marshes. This common spring sound, with its hollow quality and increasing pace, comes from the vibration of the Common Snipe's stiff tail feathers as this abundant shorebird dives through its aerial display.

Although our meetings with Common Snipes are most often auditory encounters, this well-camouflaged bird occasionally reveals itself. Its long, straight bill, squat body and heavy streaking separate it from other shorebirds. Although Common Snipes can be seen perched atop fenceposts near marshes, to fully experience this bird you must spend an evening at a marsh and listen as it cuts a melody from the spring air.

Spotted Sandpiper
Actitis macularia

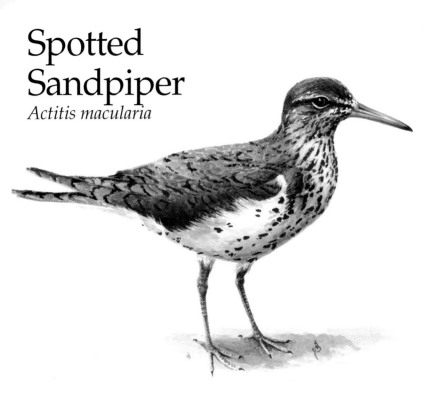

   This common shorebird of our lakes and rivers has a most uncommon mating strategy. In a reversal of the gender roles of most birds, female Spotted Sandpipers compete for male mates in spring. After the nest is built and the eggs are laid, the female leaves to find another mate and the male incubates the eggs. This is repeated up to five times before the female settles down with one male to raise the chicks.

   Spotted Sandpipers are readily identified by their arthritic, stiff-winged flight low over the water. They're easily approached, and you can often get close enough to see their spotted breast.

Marbled Godwit
Limosa fedoa

If you are right in your identification of this duck-sized prairie shorebird it will let you know with a loud and often-repeated *cor-rect cor-rect cor-rect*. Marbled Godwits have a long, two-toned, slightly upturned bill that allows them to pick off small invertebrates deep in the grass and to probe deep into prairie mud flats for soft-bodied invertebrates.

Rather than distracting predators from their nest with broken-wing tricks, Marbled Godwits prefer a more aggressive approach— dive-bombing. The angered parent will hurl itself at an intruder's head, veering off just before impact. The Marbled Godwit's lance-like bill is hard for even the most focused intruder to ignore, and it only takes a few close calls before the intruder retreats.

Long-billed Curlew
Numenius americanus

    This regal, duck-sized sandpiper of the Great Plains is often found foraging far from water in completely open prairie. Although the Long-billed Curlew seems perfectly adapted to aquatic life, its long bill and legs are equally suited to the waves of grass. The long, down-curved bill gives the curlew a dexterous tool with which to pick off grasshoppers while keeping its eyes above the top of the grass.

    The Long-billed Curlew has suffered from the cultivation of native grasslands. It's now listed as threatened in Canada and the United States, and it's restricted to isolated parcels of native prairie, where the presence of a single pair can dominate the endless landscape.

American Avocet

Recurvirostra americana

This dainty prairie shorebird is the most elegant creature breeding on the Great Plains. Although American Avocets can occur in abundance, their attractive styling should never be undervalued by prairie residents, who alone see these birds in their full breeding splendor.

The colour and structure of the American Avocet's features strike an idyllic balance between extravagance and practicality. Its graceful, upturned bill is used to skim invertebrates from the surface of prairie wetlands, where American Avocets are commonly seen wading knee-deep. Their long blue legs end in partially webbed feet, which allow avocets to swim across deep areas.

Swainson's Hawk *Buteo swainsoni*

Swainson's Hawk is the most common raptor of the open prairies. Like Turkey Vultures, Swainson's Hawks hold their slightly pointed wings in a shallow 'V' as they soar, but the dark flight feathers and white wing lining are unique to the Swainson's Hawk. The chestnut 'bib' of many Swainson's Hawks seems to complement their ravenous appetite for mice, voles and prairie snakes.

Swainson's Hawk is most common in open prairies where trees are scarce. Some of the remaining trees in this habitat are likely to contain large stick nests, which may have been used by generations of Swainson's Hawk or other raptors. Swainson's Hawk is one of the few birds to have increased breeding opportunities as a result of cultivation, but it continues to face many threats while overwintering in South America.

Red-tailed Hawk

Buteo jamaicensis

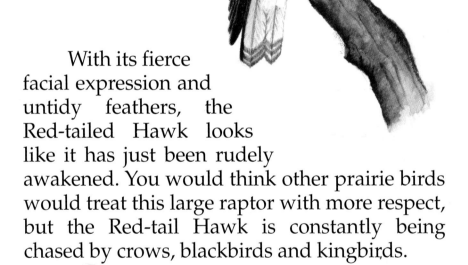

With its fierce facial expression and untidy feathers, the Red-tailed Hawk looks like it has just been rudely awakened. You would think other prairie birds would treat this large raptor with more respect, but the Red-tail Hawk is constantly being chased by crows, blackbirds and kingbirds.

Red-tailed Hawks are well named, but it's not until their second or third year that their tail becomes brick-red. The black 'belt' around the mid-section, and a dark leading edge to the wings are better field marks because they're seen in most Red-tailed Hawks of all ages. Look for these common hawks in areas of open country with nearby woodlands.

Bald Eagle
Haliaeetus leucocephalus

The Bald Eagle, the national emblem of the United States, rarely breeds on the northern prairies, but it often associates with large concentrations of migrating or wintering waterfowl. It takes four or five years for a Bald Eagle to acquire its distinctive white tail and head, but younger birds are easily recognized by their two-metre (6 ½-foot) wingspan.

Bald eagles are adept at catching fish, which they pluck from just below the water's surface, but they're not above stealing a meal from other birds. In many areas, piracy and scavenging make up the bulk of a Bald Eagle's diet. During prairie winters, Bald Eagles are often seen along open rivers and industrial cooling ponds, where they look for weak and injured ducks.

Peregrine Falcon

Falco peregrinus

The Peregrine Falcon is considered the fastest animal in the world, and it can reach speeds of up to 290 km/h (170 mph). Even the fastest ducks have little chance of escaping this effective predator. The Peregrine Falcon plunges on a victim from above, punches it in mid-air and follows it to the ground, where it kills and eats its prey.

Peregrine Falcons are among the birds most seriously affected by the use of agricultural pesticides, such as DDT, which accumulate in their bodies and reduce their breeding efficiency. The Peregrine Falcon has recovered considerably since the ban of these pesticides in the 1970s, and many pairs now nest in prairie cities and formerly occupied steep cliffs. Unfortunately, many are still exposed to these toxic chemicals when they winter in South America.

American Kestrel

Falco sparverius

This small, noisy falcon is a common sight over much of the northern prairies. It has adapted well to rural life, and it's commonly seen perched on power lines as it watches for unwary grasshoppers, birds and rodents. When not perched, American Kestrels may be seen hovering above their potential prey.

The nests of American Kestrels are often built in abandoned woodpecker cavities. Conservationists have recently discovered that kestrels will use nest boxes when natural cavities are unavailable. Its small size and rust-coloured back separates the American Kestrel from the larger falcons found on the prairies.

Merlin *Falco columbarius*

This speedy falcon is named after the famous wizard of King Arthur's court, and males are draped in a grey-blue cape. Like all falcons, Merlins are skilled hunters with pointed wings and a sleek design that enable them to pursue birds in flight.

Merlins are not naturally abundant on the prairies, but their numbers are increasing with the growth of prairie cities. They nest in older trees and have benefited from the planting of spruce trees in the neighbourhoods, parks and cemeteries of cities. Merlins are occasionally seen visiting backyard feeders, not for the nutritious seeds, but for the House Sparrows they attract.

Northern Harrier

Circus cyaneus

This common prairie hawk can best be identified by its behaviour. No other prairie raptor is so often seen flying low over fields and pastures. The slow, lazy wingbeats of a Northern Harrier coincide with its bouncy, erratic flight pattern. Unlike other hawks, which can only find their prey visually, the Northern Harrier stays close to the ground to listen for the birds, voles and mice on which it preys.

All harriers have a distinctive white rump. Females and young Northern Harriers are predominantly brown, and males are dressed in grey. These long-tailed and long-winged hawks nest on the ground in long grasses, shrubs and wet meadows.

Common Nighthawk

Chordeiles minor

This common prairie bird, which is unrelated to true hawks, has two distinct personalities—by day it rests on the ground or along a horizontal tree branch, its colour and shape blending perfectly into the texture of the bark, and at dusk it takes on a new form as a dazzling and erratic flyer that catches insects in flight.

The fascinating courtship of Common Nighthawks can be seen over prairie coulees and many eastern prairie towns. The nighthawks repeatedly call out with a loud nasal *peeent* as they fly upwards. Then they dive swiftly towards the ground and create a hollow *boom* by thrusting their wings forward at the last moment and pulling out of the dive.

Great Horned Owl

Bubo virginianus

This common night-time hunter is among the most formidable of prairie predators. Great Horned Owls use both their specialized hearing and their human-sized eyes to hunt mice, rabbits, pheasants, amphibians and occasionally fish. They have a poorly developed sense of smell, however, which may be why they're the only consistent predators of skunks. Worn out and discarded Great Horned Owl feathers are therefore often identifiable by a simple sniff.

The deep, resonant hooting of the Great Horned Owl, the provincial bird of Alberta, is most commonly heard during late winter, and it indicates that they have already begun nesting.

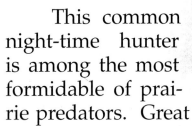

Burrowing Owl

Athene cunicularia

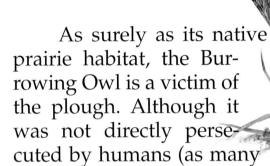

As surely as its native prairie habitat, the Burrowing Owl is a victim of the plough. Although it was not directly persecuted by humans (as many larger raptors were), the expansion of farming activities has severely reduced the population of Burrowing Owls, and it is now the most endangered of our prairie birds.

Most Burrowing Owls live in open areas of lightly grazed native prairie and nest in burrows abandoned by badgers, ground squirrels, prairie dogs or jackrabbits. They lay up to 10 eggs and raise their broods on grasshoppers and small mice. The continued cultivation of native prairies, the eradication of burrowing mammals and the contamination of their food sources have combined to yield a dark future for the Burrowing Owl.

Short-eared Owl *Asio flammeus*

The Short-eared Owl's deep, lazy flapping makes this mid-sized owl look more like a giant bat than a bird. Near dawn and dusk on the prairies, this predator of mice and voles is commonly seen perched on fenceposts or flying absent-mindedly over grassy meadows and marshes, as it looks and listens for prey.

This owl's name is quite misleading as its 'ears' (actually nothing more than feathers) are so short that they're rarely seen. The fierce yellow eyes, rounded head and vertical streaking are its best field marks.

Snowy Owl
Nyctea scandiaca

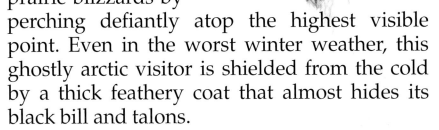

When all other animals have either migrated south or are comfortably snuggled in their winter dens, the Snowy Owl confronts the worst prairie blizzards by perching defiantly atop the highest visible point. Even in the worst winter weather, this ghostly arctic visitor is shielded from the cold by a thick feathery coat that almost hides its black bill and talons.

Snowy Owls become whiter with age and gradually lose the dark spots of their youth. Their presence on the prairies during winter depends on the availability of prey in their Arctic breeding grounds. If northern lemmings and voles are scarce, many Snowy Owls head south for the winter, and dozens of them may be seen daily on the prairies.

Turkey Vulture

Cathartes aura

The Turkey Vulture's seemingly effortless soaring is made possible by its great, silver-lined wings. Turkey Vultures seldom flap their wings, and they often rock from side to side as they fly over our prairie river valleys. The way their wings angle upwards in a shallow 'V' is a useful clue to their identification.

Turkey Vultures depend completely on dead animals (carrion) for food, and they have a highly developed sense of smell. Their heads are featherless to keep them clean and parasite-free while they dig around inside carcasses. The Turkey Vulture's habit of regurgitating its rotting meal may be a defence mechanism that allows adults to reduce their weight for a quicker take-off, and gives young vultures a powerful deterrent to would-be predators.

Ring-necked Pheasant
Phasianus colchicus

These spectacular game birds, which were introduced from Asia, are common on the northern prairies. The emerald head of the male Ringed-necked Pheasant complements its golden back and long, tapering tail. Its beauty, flavour and explosive flushing habits have made it a popular sporting bird.

Although many game birds have been introduced on the Great Plains, few have been able to tolerate the severe prairie winters. Ring-necked Pheasants are unable to migrate away from the cold, and the prairie population may suffer declines during unusually cold winters.

Gray Partridge *Perdix perdix*

This small game bird originates in Eurasia, from which its former name 'Hungarian Partridge' is derived. These birds, known locally as 'Huns,' have provided an introduction to hunting for many prairie children. Gray Partridge populations fluctuate annually but have generally increased naturally as a result of their affinity to modern agriculture.

These chunky, grey birds are often seen in small groups called 'coveys.' In winter, groups of 30 birds may be seen cuddling together for warmth. These groups form irregular circles, with all the birds' tails pointing inward, and their heads looking outward for danger.

Sharp-tailed Grouse *Tympanuchus phasianellus*

This widespread grouse used to be abundant on the prairies, but it has recently disappeared from many places. The Sharp-tailed Grouse is often incorrectly called a 'prairie chicken'—a name that properly refers to two different species, both largely absent from the northern plains.

Sharp-tailed Grouse court and breed in communal dancing grounds called 'leks.' With the purple air sacks in their necks inflated, their wings drooped and their sharp tails held high, the males dance to impress the females. Dozens of birds are attracted to these traditional grounds, but only the prime males—always at the centre of the lek—earn the right to mate with the females.

American Crow *Corvus brachyrhynchos*

The American Crow is a common sight over much of the Great Plains. This large black bird's intelligence has led it into many confrontations with humans. Studies of crow behaviour have shown that they're capable of solving simple problems, which comes as no surprise to many prairie residents who have watched American Crows systematically search for garbage in sealed containers.

Rather than berating crows for their intelligence, we should admire them. The way a group of crows tumbles through the sky, performing barrel rolls and diving at one another, can only be described as play. Most birdwatchers praise the crow's abilities, not only for the enjoyment these birds bring, but also because by following the crow's loud *caw*, birders often are led to a scolded owl.

Red-winged Blackbird

Agelaius phoeniceus

The Red-winged Blackbird is boss of the cattails, and no prairie marsh is free from its loud call and aggressive nature. The male's bright red shoulders are the most important element in his often strategic and intricate displays to defend his territory from rivals. Males whose red shoulders were experimentally painted black soon lost their territories to rivals that they had previously defeated.

The female's interest lies in the nesting territory—not the individual combatants—and a male that can successfully defend a large area of dense cattails will breed with many females. After the females have built their concealed nests and laid their eggs, the male must continue his constant vigilance against intruders and predators.

Yellow-headed Blackbird

Xanthocephalus
xanthocephalus

In a perfect world, a male Yellow-headed Blackbird would have a song to complement his splendid plumage, but a spring trip to any prairie wetland will reveal the unfortunate truth when a male arches his striking head backwards and painfully produces a pathetic metallic grind.

Despite its 'song,' the Yellow-headed Blackbird, which breeds exclusively on the Great Plains, remains a spectacular bird. Its breeding behaviour is similar to its red-winged cousin. Only the males have bold plumage, while the females are well camouflaged. Yellow-headed Blackbirds leave the Great Plains surprisingly early in autumn, and they migrate through the prairies in mixed flocks during August and September.

Common Grackle *Quiscalus quiscula*

The Common Grackle is a noisy and cocky bird that prefers to feed on the ground in open areas. Bird feeders in rural areas can attract large numbers of these blackish birds, whose cranky disposition drives away most other birds. The Common Grackle is easily identified by its long tail, large bill, and dark plumage, which may shine with hues of green, purple and blue in bright light.

The Common Grackle is another poor singer. Usually while perched in a shrub, a male grackle will slowly take a deep breath that inflates its chest and causes its feathers to rise. Then the grackle closes its eyes, gives out a loud *swaaack*, and proudly poses with its bill held high.

Brown-headed Cowbird

Molothrus ater

This small black bird with a chocolate-brown head is quickly becoming one of the most hated native birds in North America. Brown-headed Cowbirds eat grain, but they're not agricultural pests; it's their treatment of other songbirds that frustrates many bird enthusiasts.

Historically, Brown-headed Cowbirds followed the bison herds, so they were constantly on the move and unable to tend a nest; instead cowbirds lay their eggs in the nests of other songbirds, which unwittingly raise the young cowbirds as their own. Unfortunately for the parasitized host, young cowbirds are very aggressive, and they out-compete their foster parent's own offspring. The ultimate blame for the parasitism of over 140 bird species lies with the expansion of agriculture and fragmentation of forests, which have significantly increased the cowbird's range.

European Starling

Sturnus vulgaris

In 1890, 60 European Starlings were introduced to New York's Central Park as part of the New York Shakespearean Society's plan to introduce to the city all the birds mentioned in their favourite author's plays.

These highly adaptable birds, which are often confused with blackbirds, have short tails and a bright yellow bill in breeding plumage. They're mostly summer residents of prairie cities, and they're continually expanding their range at the expense of native birds. Starlings are accomplished impersonators, and they can imitate the calls of Killdeers, Red-tailed Hawks and many other species that share their wintering grounds.

American Robin

Turdus migratorius

The American Robin is much more than a common backyard visitor with a flute-like voice. Prairie residents anxiously await its annual March arrival, as if the return of this distinctive bird injects them with energy to withstand the final weeks of winter.

The robin's close relationship with urbanization has given many people an insight into a bird's social and ecological role. Watching robins dash around a yard in search of worms or ripe berries is as familiar as their three-part song—*cheerily cheery-up cheerio*. The robin's springtime appearance and song, its bright blue eggs, its hatchlings' quick development, and even the occasional death, are experiences shared by its human neighbours.

Northern Oriole *Icterus galbula*

Although they are common residents of city parks and wooded coulees, Northern Orioles are seldom seen. Unlike robins, which frequent shrubs and lawns, Northern Orioles nest and feed in the tallest deciduous trees available. Their hanging, pouch-like nests, which are deceptively strong, are easily seen in bare autumn trees. A vacant nest is often the only indication that a pair of orioles summered in an area.

The male oriole's striking black and orange plumage complements his robin-like song. His slow and purposeful *peter-peter-here-here-peter* is repeated in early spring from atop tall trees. With a little experience, you will find many songs you previously attributed to robins will reveal a beautiful Northern Oriole.

Rock Dove *Columba livia*

The Rock Dove (or Pigeon) is very dependent on human society for food and shelter. This native of Europe lives in old buildings and on ledges and bridges, and it feeds primarily on waste grain. Although these common city birds appear strained when walking—their heads move back and forth with every step—few birds are as swift in flight.

It's somewhat surprising that these non-migratory birds are able to tolerate the harsh prairie winters as well as they do, but Rock Doves are perfectly woven into rural and urban life on the prairies. To withstand the coldest temperatures, they simply ruffle their feathers and crouch in a corner out of the wind.

Belted Kingfisher

Ceryle alcyon

This medium-sized bird is always associated with water. As the name suggests, kingfishers prey mostly on fish, which they catch with precise headfirst dives. A dead branch extending over calm water often serves as a suitable perch for the Belted Kingfisher to survey the fish below.

On the Great Plains, kingfishers are restricted to large rivers and lakes. They build their nests at the ends of burrows that are often dug a metre into a sandy bank. The rattling call, blue colouration and large crest are distinctive features of the Belted Kingfisher. With most prairie birds the males are more colourful, but female Belted Kingfishers are distinguished from males by the presence of a second red 'belt.'

Mountain Bluebird *Sialia currucoides*

Photographers and painters can never do justice to the colour of the male Mountain Bluebird, which is like a piece of prairie sky come to life. To fully appreciate this prairie specialty, a male must be seen in person as he sets up his territory on a crisp, early spring morning.

The Mountain Bluebird lost many of its natural nesting sites in vacant cavities to European Starlings and House Sparrows, and through the removal of dead trees from the prairies. But prairie residents rallied for this bird, and they put up thousands of nesting boxes. The Mountain Bluebird population has increased dramatically as a result, and the birds have rewarded concerned residents with their beautiful plumage.

Blue Jay
Cyanocitta cristata

Blue Jays were originally confined to the eastern hardwood forests, but they have now settled into life on the prairies as well. Their loud *jay-jay-jay* call, blue and white plumage, and large crest are familiar to anyone with sunflower seeds or peanuts at their feeder.

Blue Jays are intelligent, aggressive birds that don't hesitate to drive smaller birds, squirrels or even cats away when they feel threatened. This jay's boldness is reflected in its diet, for it will eat just about anything, including nuts, berries, insects and other bird's eggs. This flexible lifestyle has helped Blue Jays expand their range and succeed where other birds have been unable to adapt to change.

Black-billed Magpie

Pica pica

When describing a magpie, few people mention its long tail, striking, iridescent plumage and diverse vocalizations. Rather, Black-billed Magpies are labelled as loud pests that drive off other birds, wake people up with their loud, nasal *yeck-yeck-yeck* and tear into garbage.

Black-billed Magpies don't waste all of their intelligence frustrating humans, however, and they're skilled at many natural tasks. Magpies build impressive fully domed nests that are re-used by a variety of birds after the magpie abandons it. During autumn magpies bury thousands of food items in preparation for the long harsh winters. Black-billed Magpies are resourceful, adaptable and canny birds, and in many ways they possess the same pioneering spirit as the prairie's human inhabitants.

Eastern Kingbird

Tyrannus tyrannus

The Eastern Kingbird is pugnacious, and it will fearlessly attack crows, hawks and other large birds that pass through its territory. The intruders are often vigorously pursued for some distance, until the kingbird is satisfied that there is no further threat.

The Eastern Kingbird is a vocal bird, and it's easily identified by its all-black back, pure white chest and white-tipped tail. Its courtship flight, which can be seen in river valleys and shrubby areas, is characterized by short, quivering wingbeats.

Rufous-sided Towhee

Pipilo erythrophthalmus

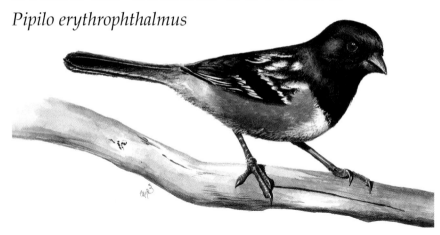

This large, cocky sparrow is most often heard in the dense understorey before it's seen. The Rufous-sided Towhee forages with a characteristic double-scratching technique that rustles dead leaves and grass beneath dense thickets. Pishing (loudly kissing the back of your hand, or puckering up and saying 'pish' as loudly and wetly as comfortable) is irresistible for towhees, and they quickly pop out from cover to investigate the curious noise.

It's difficult to misidentify a male Rufous-sided Towhee. His black hood, white chest and red flanks are characteristic of this species alone. With binoculars and bright light you can also see this bird's blood-red eyes. Although eastern Rufous-sided Towhees sing a clear *drink your teeeea*, the song of the prairie towhee has a nasal quality and ends with a buzzy trill.

Gray Catbird
Dumetella carolinensis

The Gray Catbird is a sleek, slate-grey bird that commonly displays an unusual 'mooning' behaviour, in which it raises its long, slender tail to show its chestnut undertail coverts. This behaviour, which is one of the elements of courtship, may help female catbirds choose the best mates.

The Gray Catbird is a bird of dense shrubs and thickets, and although it's relatively common in appropriate habitats, its distinctive call, rather than the bird itself, is most commonly encountered. The Gray Catbird's unmistakable cat-like 'meowing,' for which it's named, is the key to field identification.

Brown Thrasher

Toxostoma rufum

Male Brown Thrashers have the largest vocal repertoire of any prairie bird—in excess of 3,000 song types. Although thrashers don't have the sweetest voice on the prairies, their loud, continually varying songs are worth a listen. Thrashers often repeat a song twice—*drop-it drop-it, pull-it-up pull-it-up*—before moving on to another verse.

Brown Thrashers have a reddish-brown back and tail and a heavily streaked breast. They're common in thickets and shrubs, often in close proximity to humans. They're shy birds, and they need a lot of coaxing before they will come out into the open.

Northern Flicker *Colaptes auratus*

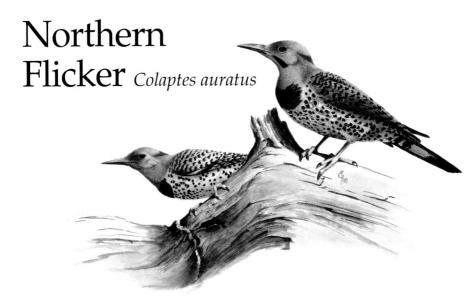

The Northern Flicker is a woodpecker, but its behaviour is often more similar to a robin's. Flickers are the most terrestrial of the North American woodpeckers, and they're often seen on the ground feeding on ants or taking a dust bath. Often, it's only when the Northern Flicker is near its nest cavity that it behaves like other woodpeckers.

The Northern Flicker has spotty plumage and a black bib, and in flight its white rump is distinctive. On the prairies, most Northern Flickers have yellow under their wings and tails, and the males have a black 'moustache.' Red-shafted Northern Flickers, which have red markings instead of yellow and a red 'moustache,' are more common west of the Continental Divide, and they used to be considered a separate species.

Cedar Waxwing

Bombycilla cedrorum

A faint high-pitched whistle is often your first clue that waxwings are around. Search the tree tops and these cinnamon-crested birds will serve up a pleasant reward. The Cedar Waxwing's body feathers are so fine that they're nearly indistinguishable from one another.

Cedar Waxwings are most often seen in large flocks in late summer, when they congregate on fruit trees and quickly eat all the berries. Cedar Waxwings are gentle birds, and their suspicious black mask in no way represents this bird's inoffensive character. During harsh winters, prairie cities are often visited by Bohemian Waxwings, a large cousin of the Cedar Waxwing identified by its rusty undertail coverts.

Mourning Dove *Zenaida macroura*

The peaceful *cooo-cooo-coooah* call of the Mourning Dove diffuses quickly through cottonwoods stands and echoes the lonely spirit of the prairies.

This native member of the pigeon family is widespread throughout the Great Plains. Mourning Doves are swift flyers, and when they explode into flight their wing-tips clap above and below their bodies. In flight these sleek, long-tailed doves fly with grace, and they're always accompanied by a faint whistling of wind through their wings.

Western Meadowlark

Sturnella neglecta

The Western Meadowlark, the voice of the Great Plains, symbolizes the open prairies. It is the state bird of Montana, Nebraska, North Dakota and others. The beauty of its song can only be fully appreciated in its natural context.

The Western Meadowlark is perfectly adapted to the landscape of the Great Plains in which it spends its summers. Its yellow chest, with its black 'V,' and white outer tail feathers serve to attract mates—and predators. But predators are easily confused when a meadowlark turns its back or folds away its white tail feathers and blends with the prairie grass.

Black-capped Chickadee *Parus atricapillus*

The Black-capped Chickadee is one of the most pleasant birds in our cities and forested areas. This exceptionally friendly bird often greets walkers along trails and welcomes them into a world of shrubs, dry leaves and insect eggs. Throughout most of the year, chickadees move about in loose flocks that surround human visitors with their delicate *chick-a-dee-dee-dee* calls.

During the summer, Black-capped Chickadees seem strangely absent from city parks and wooded ravines; they may be too busy raising their families to greet and entertain passers by. It seems that chickadees unselfishly let the flighty migrants have their way in the woods for three brief summer months, but once the first autumn chill arrives, the woods will again be theirs.

Barn Swallow

Hirundo rustica

The graceful flight of these birds is a common sight during summer. Barn Swallows build their cup-shaped mud nests in the eaves of barns and picnic shelters, and occasionally in nest boxes or any other structure that provides protection from the rain.

The Barn Swallow is easily recognized by its steel-blue back, chestnut throat and long, forked tail. Swallows are insectivorous, and they catch flying insects in mid-flight. Because Barn Swallows are often closely associated with human structures, it's not uncommon that a nervous parent will dive repeatedly at intruders to force their retreat.

Tree Swallow
Tachycineta bicolor

The population of Tree Swallows has increased during the past decades, an unforeseen result of the bluebird nest box program. These common swallows are cavity nesters, and they are among the most frequent users of nest boxes intended for bluebirds. Unlike European Starlings and House Sparrows, which actively usurp nest cavities from bluebirds, the competition from Tree Swallows results from a scarcity of nest cavities.

Tree Swallows are often observed spiralling around in large groups over open fields in early spring. They can be identified by their effortless flight and bicoloured plumage—white on the bottom and blue-green on top. Tree Swallows commonly skim low over calm water for a quick drink, leaving only a small wake behind them.

Cliff Swallow *Hirundo pyrrhonota*

Cliff Swallows aren't as widespread as Barn or Tree Swallows, but where they do occur, thousands are often encountered. Cliff Swallows (and occasionally Northern Rough-winged Swallows) nest under almost every bridge that spans our prairie rivers. If you stop and inspect the undersides of a bridge, you will see hundreds of gourd-shaped mud nests stuck to the pillars and structural beams.

Natural nesting colonies occur on sandstone overhangs and cliffs, usually along prairie rivers. The nests are meticulously made from mud, one mouthful at a time. Hundreds of Cliff Swallows busily building their nests create a chaotic scene with their constant procession back and forth between their nest and the mud flat.

Ruby-throated Hummingbird

Archilochus colubris

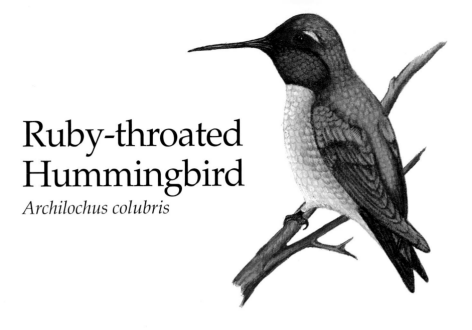

You are fortunate if you are one the few to get a prolonged look at a Ruby-throated Hummingbird, the only prairie hummingbird. Most meetings are over before they begin—a loud hum draws your attention to a small object flitting about, but it quickly disappears through the trees. It's often only after the bird has disappeared that its identification becomes apparent.

Fortunately, Ruby-throated Hummingbirds are easily attracted to feeders of sweetened water. The male's iridescent ruby throat and emerald back play with the sunlight in ever-switching colours. The Ruby-throated Hummingbird's gentle appearance is misleading; these fiercely aggressive hummingbirds will chase intruders away in a spirited defence of a food source.

Common Yellowthroat

Geothlypis trichas

This energetic warbler of the cattails is easily identified by sight or by sound. The male Common Yellowthroat's oscillating *witchety-witchety-witchety* song is not easy to forget. As this bird's name suggests, it's both common (it's the most numerous warbler in North America) and yellow-throated. The male's characteristic black mask is an unmistakable field mark.

Female yellowthroats are rarely seen because they keep their nests deep within the thick vegetation surrounding prairie marshes. Although Common Yellowthroats are among the most common hosts of cowbird eggs, a stable and productive breeding population protects them from any declines.

Yellow Warbler

Dendroica petechia

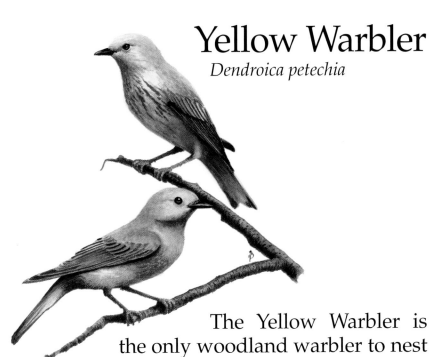

The Yellow Warbler is the only woodland warbler to nest over much of the prairies. Although the Yellow Warbler is common in woodlands throughout our region, a glimpse at one is always a sweet surprise. The male's brilliant yellow plumage contrasts sharply with his fine red chest streaks. The Yellow Warbler is often inaccurately called a wild canary because of both its yellow colour and its lively *sweet sweet sweet I'm so so sweet* courtship song.

Unlike most other species parasitized by cowbirds, Yellow Warblers either abandon their nest or simply build another nest atop the old eggs. In true warbler fashion, the Yellow Warbler is active and inquisitive, and it flits from branch to branch in search of juicy caterpillars, aphids and beetles.

American Goldfinch *Carduelis tristis*

The American Goldfinch is a bright, cheery songbird that is commonly seen in weedy fields, roadsides and backyards, where it often feeds on thistle seeds. The male's black cap and wings separate it from the other yellow prairie birds that are also mistakenly called wild canaries. The American Goldfinch delays nesting until June to ensure a dependable source of thistles and dandelion seeds to feed its young.

The American Goldfinch is absent from much of the prairies during winter, and it migrates in large flocks as far south as Mexico. When it returns in late spring, the American Goldfinch swings over fields in its distinctive, undulating flight, and it fills the air with its jubilant call—*po-ta-to-chip.*

Chestnut-collared Longspur

Calcarius ornatus

The Chestnut-collared Longspur is one of the easiest grassland buntings to identify as it flushes from the ditches and fields of the prairies. The males are the only black buntings of the open prairies that show a small black triangle on an otherwise white tail. Chestnut-collared Longspurs are occasionally seen singing atop fenceposts or boulders above the sea of grass.

The flashy Chestnut-collared Longspur is a symbol of native grassland. As these areas have turned to wheat fields, Longspurs have continually declined and are now restricted to treeless, uncultivated areas. Although this bird may never attain its former abundance, its exuberant habits are not uncommon in favourable habitats.

Lark Bunting
Calamospiza melanocorys

The fluttering aerial courtship display of Lark Buntings can be easily confused with that of a large butterfly. Male Lark Buntings fly straight up, pause and then float to the ground like a falling leaf. During this oft-repeated flight, the male's bell-like voice tinkles above the prairie chorus.

The Lark Bunting's name is on the long list of declining species on our native prairies. Like so many other birds, the Lark Bunting requires open natural fields and sagebrush flats. Its courtship reflects its association to the Great Plains before cultivation, roads and fenceposts. Because there were no high points from which to sing, the Lark Bunting has always delivered its song on the wing.

Snow Bunting
Plectrophenax nivalis

Once the breeding songbirds have gone and the first winter storm has blanketed the northern prairies, Snow Buntings arrive from the Arctic and settle in for winter. Thousands congregate in windswept fields and scratch at the frozen soil to uncover grain left over from autumn.

During winter, Snow Buntings are rarely seen alone. Their large flocks are accustomed to the ground, because Snow Buntings spend all of their lives in areas where there are few areas to perch. On a cold winter day, it is a special treat to watch a flock of Snow Buntings, often numbering in the thousands, rise up in unison. Their black and white plumage gives the illusion that the flock is appearing and disappearing against the snowy backdrop.

White-breasted Nuthatch

Sitta carolinensis

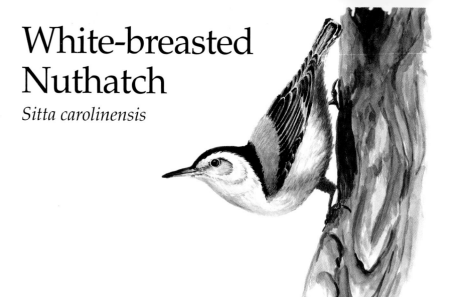

This common year-round resident of deciduous forests has a precarious foraging habit. Unlike all other birds that forage by moving *up* tree trunks, nuthatches move *down* trunks headfirst. They occasionally stop with their head held out at a right angle to the trunk. By moving down the tree, White-breasted Nuthatches are able to find seeds, insects and nuts that are overlooked by woodpeckers.

Although the White-breasted Nuthatch may look like a woodpecker, its feeding habits, white cheek and blue-grey back should prevent any confusion. Bird feeders in older communities near mature forests will often attract White-breasted Nuthatches during winter. Their distinctive nasal *yank-yank-yank* call is heard increasingly as spring arrives.

Downy Woodpecker

Picoides pubescens

The black and white Downy Woodpecker is the smallest and most common woodpecker in wooded ravines and city parks. It's easily attracted to backyard feeders by suet (beef fat from around the kidneys). Males are easily distinguished from females by a small patch of red feathers at the back of the head.

Although the Downy Woodpecker is the most common woodpecker, its close relative, the Hairy Woodpecker, should also be familiar. The Hairy Woodpecker is nearly identical in plumage to the Downy, but it is almost twice as large. Also, the Hairy Woodpecker's chisel-like bill is as long as its head is wide, while the Downy Woodpecker's bill is comparatively shorter.

House Sparrow
Passer domesticus

This common backyard bird often confuses novice birdwatchers because it can be very nondescript. The male is relatively conspicuous—he has a black bib, a grey cap and white lines trailing down from his mouth (as though he had spilled milk on himself)—but the best field mark for the females is that there are no field marks.

House Sparrows were introduced in the 1850s to control insects. Although these familiar birds consume great quantities of insects, they have become a major pest. The House Sparrow's aggressive nature usurps several native songbirds from nesting cavities. The House Sparrow is now the most common bird in cities and farms, and it is a constant reminder of human influence on natural systems.

American Tree Sparrow

Spizella arborea

The American Tree Sparrow's annual flood through the Great Plains in early spring and late autumn is a sign of the changing seasons. For a few weeks, these migrants decorate the leafless rural shrublands like ornaments on a Christmas tree. As the first songbirds to appear in March and the last to leave the prairies in late October, American Tree Sparrows quietly announce the opening of spring and the closing of autumn.

These humble sparrows often go unnoticed despite their large numbers. American Tree Sparrows occasionally visit city feeders during their migrations and as winter residents in southern Canada and the northern prairie states. The dull red cap and central chest spot are simple field marks for the American Tree Sparrow.

Song Sparrow *Melospiza melodia*

What surprises are produced by this bird! The Song Sparrow's drab plumage doesn't prepare you for the symphonic song of this common sparrow. Although the Song Sparrow ends its tunes with a prolonged melody, it always begins with three sharp *hip-hip-hip* notes.

This summer resident of the Great Plains prefers shrubby areas often close to water. The Song Sparrow is also commonly heard at dawn and at dusk in ravines and city parks. Although this sparrow's plumage doesn't complement its song, the effort that the Song Sparrow extends in its delivery is commendable.

White-throated Sparrow

Zonotrichia albicollis

The White-throated Sparrow is a migrant over much of our area, and it treats us to its clear distinctive song for only a few weeks in spring. Despite this brief exposure, the White-throated Sparrow's distinctive *Ohhhh dear sweet Canada Canada Canada* song is well recognized.

Aside from its characteristic call, White-throated Sparrows are often observed during migration and occasionally throughout winter. A steady source of bird seed in the winter will provide a reliable food source for an otherwise doomed White-throated Sparrow that has failed to migrate. This sparrow is a blessing to most city bird feeders, and its striped head and white throat allow this northern breeder to stand out from the many House Sparrows.

Savannah Sparrow
Passerculus sandwichensis

The Savannah Sparrow is a common bird of the open country. Its dull brown plumage, with a streaked breast, conceals it perfectly in the long grasses of the native prairies, farms and roadsides. It's most often seen darting across roads, highways and open fields to escape intruders. Savannah Sparrows resort to flight only as a last alternative; they prefer to run swiftly and inconspicuously through the long grass. The Savannah Sparrow's distinctive song—*tea-tea-tea-teeeea-today*—and the yellow patch in front of its eyes are the best ways to distinguish it from the many other grassland sparrows.

The Vesper Sparrow is distinguished from the Savannah Sparrow only by its chestnut shoulder and white outer tail feathers. Fortunately the songs of these two sparrows are very different. The Vesper Sparrow concludes its song with a short musical trill, and it starts with four distinctive notes—*ve-ve-sper-sper*.

Horned Lark

Eremophila alpestris

The Horned Lark is a very common bird and is often seen trying to outrun approaching cars along gravel roads, before finally taking to flight. This small songbird's first instinct is to run rather than fly, and the speeds it can attain on foot are quite remarkable. Although the Horned Lark's running strategy is distinctive, as are its 'face mask' and 'sideburn' markings, its black tail is unique among prairie songbirds, and it is unmistakable as it flies out of harm's way.

Horned Larks are found in every type of unforested area—tundra, clearcuts in northern forests, mountain tops, sea coasts, and open fields and grasslands of the prairies. In areas of the prairies where Horned Larks don't overwinter, they are among the first songbirds to arrive in late March.

Red-eyed
Vireo *Vireo olivaceus*

The Red-eyed Vireo is the undisputed champion of singing endurance. During breeding seasons, males sing from tall deciduous trees throughout the day. Most songbirds stop their courting melodies five or six hours after sunrise, but the Red-eyed Vireo seems to gain momentum as the day progresses. Its robin-like voice is distinctive, and it's best paraphrased as *look-up way-up tree-top see-me here-I-am*. A patient ornithologist estimated that the energetic Red-eyed Vireo sings this memorable phrase up to 10,000 times a day.

Visual identification of the Red-eyed Vireo is much harder, since its olive-brown colour conceals it well among the foliage of deciduous trees. Although this vireo does indeed have a red eye, this feature can only be seen through powerful binoculars in excellent light conditions.

Least Flycatcher

Empidonax minimus

Fortunately for birders, the Least Flycatcher's song is much more distinctive than its plumage. When you enter any young deciduous stand in spring, the Least Flycatcher's chipper *che-bec* is usually the first identifiable sound you'll hear. If you follow this sharp song to its source you will find a small, slim bird patiently waiting for insects to fly into range.

Flycatchers are well named, and they often catch flying insects from a favourite perch. As they 'hawk' or 'sallie'—terms used to describe their habit of leaving a perch to snatch up a flying insect and then quickly returning to the same perch—Least Flycatchers can be quite entertaining.

Marsh Wren *Cistothorus palustris*

This energetic little bird is always associated with dense cattail marshes. Although it prefers to keep a low profile by staying hidden in the deep vegetation, its distinctive song is one of the characteristic voices of our prairie wetlands. This small, heavily streaked bird's song has the same repetitive quality of an old sewing machine. Once you learn the simple song, you are unable to avoid hearing it when you visit suitable Marsh Wren habitats.

A typical sighting of a Marsh Wren is usually nothing more than a brown blur moving noisily about deep within the cattails. Although the wren may be less than three metres from the observer, its cryptic habits and appearance are frustratingly effective. Patient observers may be rewarded with a brief glimpse of a Marsh Wren perching high atop a cattail reed as it quickly evaluates its territory.

House Wren *Troglodytes aedon*

This common bird of suburbs, city parks and woodlands sings as though its lungs are bottomless. The sweet warbling song of the House Wren, surpassed only by the Winter Wren, is distinguished by its melodious tone and its uninterrupted endurance. Although the House Wren is far smaller than a sparrow, in just one breath it offers an unending song.

Like all wrens, the House Wren often carries its tail cocked straight up. Bird houses will often attract a pair of House Wrens to your backyard, where they will reward you with their beautiful song and their ravenous appetite for insects. House Wrens can be aggressive to one another. They are often displaced from their nests by European Starlings and House Sparrows, which don't respect this bird's musical virtues.

Watching Birds

Getting started at birdwatching needn't cost a lot of money. Many people get a lot of pleasure by simply putting out household scraps on a homemade feeder that is close enough to a window so that the birds can be easily seen as they come and go.

Most people interested in birdwatching use a pair of binoculars, as this lets them identify key bird characteristics, such as plumage, leg colour and bill shape. Binoculars will also allow you to observe timid birds that normally stay at a distance or in the cover of bushes and trees. Small details help build the over-all picture of a bird, which helps identify the species.

Buying binoculars is probably the largest financial commitment a birdwatcher will make, but it isn't necessary to spend a great deal of money, as there are some inexpensive but good models available. Shopping for binoculars can be confusing, and much has been written about how to choose a pair. The best advice is to ask a birdwatcher or to talk to someone at a nature centre. Remember that no one pair will be perfect for every situation—birdwatching in woodlands requires binoculars with a wide field of view and a reasonably low magnification (8x is probably best), while watching shorebirds in a wetland requires a higher magnification, and a telescope would then be useful. Binoculars tend to get heavy hanging around your neck, and this should be kept in mind when you're selecting a pair. A wide neck strap certainly helps, but if you have a choice, you won't regret buying the lightest pair that seems to be right for you.

Aside from binoculars, the only other piece of equipment you will need is a book to help you identify the birds you see. Armed with a pair of binoculars and a field guide, you will find a whole new world opening up for you as you take advantage of the many excellent birdwatching sites in your area. Soon you will be taking your binoculars with you on a hike or when you walk your dog in the park— the opportunities for their use are endless.

Keeping bird notes

Keeping records of the birds you see in your backyard and on excursions will provide you with many hours of pleasure. A daily or weekly checklist of sightings will tell you a great deal about avian visitors in your area—it will provide a record of how numbers change through the seasons and from year to year and of specific migration times of many species. You'll soon know when to expect the first

Western Meadowlark of spring or the first Snow Bunting of autumn.

Also keep notes on the birds' behaviour to build up profiles of individual species. Do they 'hawk' for insects from a snag on the forest edge? Do they like a shrubby canopy that provides continuous shelter, or are they usually seen on tree tops?

Try to record a clear image of what the bird looked like. A simple line sketch is ideal, and it really doesn't matter how artistic it is! Include as much information as you can about the bird—its plumage characteristics, its bill and leg colour, sounds it makes and other behavioural characteristics.

Keep your records in a notebook to avoid losing them. If you intend to take your notebook on hikes, make sure it has a soft, waterproof cover, which will let you stuff it into your pocket or pack and will protect it from the rain. A useful tip: pencils are easier to sketch with than pens, and they write more easily on damp paper.

Another good way to learn about birds is to join your local natural history or bird society. You will meet many knowledgeable people who will be happy to teach you what they know about birds and to show you the best places to see them in various areas. Many organizations run field trips to some of the good birdwatching spots, and they provide the benefit of an expert to help with identification problems. Christmas Bird Counts are a highlight for birdwatchers, regardless of skill level. Look for information on these in your local paper.

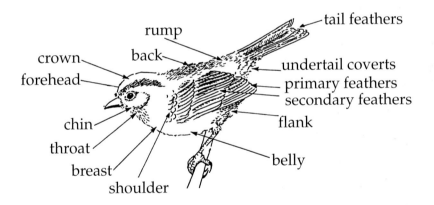

tail feathers

rump

crown

back

forehead

undertail coverts

primary feathers

secondary feathers

chin

flank

throat

breast

belly

shoulder

Bird Feeders

Why bother putting up a bird feeder in your backyard? The great advantage is that if you feed birds on a regular basis they learn to come to that spot every day, and as more birds learn about your feeder, the numbers of species and individuals increase. Don't expect the birds to find your feeder immediately, however. It often takes a few weeks for the numbers of visiting birds to build up, so persevere and be patient, and your backyard can become your own bird sanctuary.

Feeders also provide advantages for birds, and they are used much more frequently when natural food sources are less abundant, particu-

larly in the winter months. When the weather gets colder, the birds using neighbourhood feeders may rely on this food source for survival. Late autumn is a good time to establish a feeder, as that's when birds are setting up their winter territories.

Once you have started feeding birds, you should keep it up throughout the winter, particularly during the colder weather. A break in the routine could well mean the that the birds you've so carefully attracted will move on or won't survive. Try feeding the birds at the same time each day and you'll see how quickly they adjust to a routine. Early morning is best. It's also good to provide enough food to last two or three days.

There may be only a few birds at your feeder at any one time, but this doesn't mean that only a few birds are using the feeder. It can be difficult to recognize individual birds, but studies with banded birds have shown that birds use feeders for only short periods during the day. Any one feeder may be visited by many individuals throughout the daylight hours as they forage through the neighbourhood.

It is best to put your feeder some distance from the house, but within easy view of a window, because the birds will be wary if they see movement. Find a site that will likely be attractive to birds, such as immediately adjacent to dense trees and bushes, rather than in the middle of a lawn. The availability of escape cover is just as important as the food itself. Small birds are innately aware of the dangers of avian predators, such as hawks, and they will soon take a liking to a feeder that offers safety as well as good food.

Also remember that cats are a real threat to birds, and try to make it more difficult for cats to sneak up on birds at your feeder. Avoid putting your feeder right beside a low bush or another suitable hiding place for cats, and make sure the feeder is high enough to be out of reach of even the most agile cat, which can leap as high as two metres. Also, a large circle of page wire under your feeder will soon dissuade cats.

Seasons of Birdwatching

Spring

Although the American Robin is the traditional and much celebrated harbinger of spring, there are a number of birds that may precede it to cheer in the lengthening days, including the Western Meadowlark, whose song is a clear note of fresh promise.

As soon as there is the first sign of spring break-up and the chance for an edge of water in the shallow ponds, look for Killdeers and Ring-billed Gulls and listen for the haunting call of Canada Geese far overhead. Horned Larks are also among the early arrivals.

Soon after the robin, the flights of returning migrants will begin to flood through the prairies. Late spring, when trees are just beginning to leaf out and the birds are in full breeding colours, is an excellent time for birdwatching.

Summer

This is the time of nesting birds, and the year-round residents are augmented by the scores of species that find the prairies an ideal nesting area. Identification of birds takes on a diminished importance as their territorial

enthusiasm and courtship antics become the centre of attention. For those who have the foresight to set up nesting boxes or the good fortune to have some of their trees selected as nesting sites, the hours of early summer can be richly occupied in watching as the eggs hatch and the fledglings begin their development.

Autumn

From late summer on, the return migration is underway. It is the most likely time to see the largest variety of species. Migrants that flew quickly over the prairies in the spring now rest and feed in fields and food-rich woodlands. Uncommon birds are likely to be sighted in any backyard and they are almost certain to be found in those with a dense growth of both shrubs and trees.

Late summer and early autumn produce a rich variety of bird life as the many adults, pre-occupied with raising young during the summer, now wander over larger areas. The young, which in many species are now independent, will also be foraging much more widely prior to migration.

As the daylight hours diminish, large flocks of waterfowl begin to be seen and heard overhead. Although any watcher is tempted to melancholy at the sight of flocks winging south, it is an ideal time for birdwatching expeditions to a nearby lake or wetland to view the marshalling of the flights.

Winter

A number of birds remain and a few even arrive for winter. For those willing to locate a variety of feeders and suet bags around the yard, it will be a rare day when no birds arrive. Winter birdwatching will not reveal many species, but the species encountered will command respect as chickadees, nuthatches, and owls are hardy and resilient to our long cold winters.

Recommended Reading

Field Guides

Field Guide to the Birds of North America. S.L. Scott, ed. National Geographic Society, Washington, D.C.

Birds of North America: A Guide to Field Identification. Chandler S. Robbins, Bertel Bruun, Herbert S. Zim. Golden Press, New York.

Western Birds. Roger Tory Peterson. Houghton Mifflin Company, Boston.

Birder's Guide to Southwestern Manitoba. Calvin W. Cuthbert, J.I. Horton, M.W. McCowan, B.G. Robinson, and N.G. Short. Brandon Natural History Society, Brandon, Manitoba.

Birds of Edmonton. Robin Bovey. Lone Pine Publishing, Edmonton.

Birds of Calgary. Robin Bovey. Lone Pine Publishing, Edmonton.

Reference Books

The Birder's Handbook: A Field Guide to the Natural History of North American Birds. P. Ehrlich, D. Dobkin, D. Wheye. Simon and Shuster, Toronto.

The Birds of Alberta. W. Ray Salt and Jim R. Salt. Hurtig Publishers, Edmonton.

The Audubon Society Master Guide to Birding. John Farrand Jr., ed. National Audubon Society. Knoft, New York.

The Birds of Canada. Revised edition. Earl W. Godfrey. National Museum of Natural Sciences, Ottawa.

Birds of the Great Plains. Paul A. Johnsgard. University of Nebraska Press, Lincoln.

The Atlas of Breeding Birds of Alberta. Glen P. Semenchuk, ed. Federation of Alberta Naturalists, Edmonton.

Birding Magazines

Birder's World. Holland, Michigan.

Bird Watcher's Digest. Marietta, Ohio.

Wild Bird. Irving, California.

Birds of the Wild. Markham, Ontario.

Index

S

T

About the Author

Chris Fisher is in the Department of Renewable Resources at the University of Alberta, where he studies endangered species management and wildlife interpretation. His enthusiasm for wildlife has allowed him to personally witness much of the diversity of life that occurs on the Great Plains, through consulting projects and directed recreational activities. As a photographer and a lab instructor for a wildlife course, Chris has had the pleasure of sharing his wildlife experiences with others, and he strives to foster a greater appreciation of wildlife values.